KE1

When Infidelity Strikes

Dr. Christine Rice Slocumb

Skill of Success & Associates, Inc.   2014   Land O' Lakes, FL
www.SkillofSuccess.net

KEEPING IT REAL

Copyright © 2014 by Dr. Christine Rice Slocumb
Published by Skill of Success & Associates, Inc.

All rights reserved. No part of this book may be reproduced or transmitted in any form or by any means without written permission of the author. Exceptions are made for brief excerpts to be used in published reviews. For information about permission to reproduce selections of this book, write to Permissions, Skill of Success & Associates, Inc., 3230 Prairie Iris Drive, Land O' Lakes, FL 34638

ISBN-13: 978-1494844165

ISBN-10: 1494844168

This publication is designed to provide accurate and authoritative information with regard to the subject matter covered. It is sold with the understanding that the publisher is not engaged in rendering legal, career, accounting, or other professional advice. If legal or other expert assistance is required, the services of a competent professional person should be sought.

This book is available at quantity discounts for bulk purchases.
For information, please call (478) 714-8262.

Our home page is at
www.KeepingItRealBook.com

Early Praise for Keeping It Real

The title of this book, *Keeping it Real* captures the pure essence of its context. It is a must-read for all women who have experienced any form of disappointment, hurt or betrayal in a relationship. Though the testimony shared wraps itself around the story of marriage, I feel this book to be relevant not only for those who are married but also for those who are in any type of serious relationship. It is real, it is pure, and it is liberating….the words you read are anointed to set the captive free! Indeed, within these pages are steps to "healing and freedom"…. It's yours if you want it; all you have to do is read, believe, receive and begin the process. - **Minister Julie Dumas Morris**

As you read this book, *Keeping It Real,* you will find words truly from the Lord through Christine Rice. You will find out you're not the only woman who has been abused, and as my mother would say, "You will not be the last one." I thank God for Christine's willingness to tell it like it is! - **Pastor Pamela Davis**

Christine Rice Slocumb flings open the door on a subject which has too long been closeted away. Churches in particular have shrunk from openly addressing the issues of infidelity and abuse among Christians. Christine takes a no-holds-barred approach to this sensitive topic and speaks from a heart which has been broken by experience. However, this book does not stop there. To those in similar circumstances—past or present—Christine offers encouragement to take action when warranted and renew commitment when possible. She includes poetry to inspire and prayers to heal. If you have been victimized by infidelity, this book offers common-sense advice and sincere, prayerful support for your journey of healing. - **Wendie Brannen, Licensed Clinical Social Worker & Editor**

Chris, WOW! Your book is excellent and inspiring. I could not stop reading. I saw myself in your pain and in your deliverance. Every woman who reads your book will relate. Praises and glory to GOD for many of those women whom will be set free. I love you Christine Slocumb and I very much enjoyed Ronnie's testimony on his Ruth. GOD bless you my sister and this book is just the beginning of your writer's career. Thank you for sharing and allowing me to be a part of your book and your journey. I praise GOD for you. Love you infinitely my sister. - **Betty Toussaint**

Dedication

This piece of work is first and foremost dedicated to The Father, Son and Holy Spirit. Without the Trinity's work on my behalf, where would I be?

To my Boaz, my husband Ronnie Slocumb. Wow! I prayed and God sent me you. He gave me everything I asked for in a husband and so much more. How cool is that! Every time I look at you I am amazed of how God put us together. He did it His way so that only He could get the Glory. Every time I look at you I see Jesus operating in you and through you. Your love is so pure and genuine. Thank you for loving me as Christ loves the church. Next to God, I am forever yours.

To my children, TyRone & Teranesha, I love you both with all my heart. God blessed me with two remarkable children. Thank you for loving me in spite of all the ups and mostly downs that I took you through while going through my own journeys. May God continue to smile upon you both, and may your marriage always be blessed and filled with the joy, peace, happiness, good health, wealth and prosperity that God has intended for marriage.

To my best sister-friend Julie, oh my gosh! I am so glad that God joined us together as friends. Thank you for all the talks, the laughs, and the crying together. Thank you for keeping it real and being that honest friend that so many people lack in their lives. You walked with me through my journey. I walked with you through yours. I love the fact that we always take time to share, know and understand what is going on in each other's lives. We never express disapproval, judge, or make each other feel ashamed or unworthy because of something we may have done or did not do.

We embrace life head on and are true to our feelings and purpose that God has for us and hold each other accountable to reach the mark of the high calling. Chains no longer keep us bound, we are free. May God continue to make your way and marriage prosperous in every area of your life. You are truly an awesome woman of God, and I love you!

Dedication goes to each person who constantly reminded me to finish this book. You know who you are. A word of encouragement goes a long way. I am honored to have such true friends in my inner circle. Much love to you. Know that God has a purpose and plan for your life and go for it! Much love.

To every person who has or may be walking through a process where unfaithfulness has affected your life, my heart feels your pain and tears. Know that you are never alone, the hand of God is with you, He loves you, and joy really does come in the morning!

CONTENT

Introduction	8
Broken Beyond Pieces	10
Episode I: What???	11
Emotions	15
Episode II: Now That I Know, What Should I Do?	17
The Silence of God	20
Episode III: My Journey (Personal Testimony)	21
Shhhhhhhhh	29
Episode IV: Shhhhhhh It's a Secret	30
"Typical Man"	34
Episode V: "Typical Man" Not Accepted	35
Soul Ties	42
Free to Be	53
Hello ME	55
Women of Great Value	77

Introduction

Warning: This book may offend some, but that is not the intent. If this book is in your hand, do not put it down. You were led to it by Holy Spirit, because of where you are walking in this season of your life. One of life's hardest challenges is to find out your husband has been unfaithful. This book is written from a woman's perspective because of where I have walked in my life. (I do know for a fact that there are also women out there who are unfaithful to their husbands; therefore, men, if you happen to read this book, any place where you see that it is talking about unfaithful men, just plug in "women" if you are dealing with an unfaithful wife.) If you are the one that is conducting such unfaithful behavior, male or female, then you should stop! *Just Keeping It Real.*

The word *unfaithful* can mean different things to different people, but the bottom line is, somewhere, somehow trust has been broken, hearts have been ripped out, and families, children, friends and ministries have all been infected. Yes, I said "infected" because unfaithfulness is like an infectious, deadly disease. It hurts and may even kill you as well as those around you.

As you read this book, may Father God protect your mind by giving you peace and understanding. I pray that Holy Spirit will guide your every footstep while you walk out your process and get your fire back!

I pray that every broken place in your heart will be mended and every tear you have cried in sadness be captured by the hands of Jesus and turned into unspeakable joy.

Keeping It Real: When Infidelity Strikes

God is so awesome that he knows your heart, your every thought and your desires. He is the one Who put the desires in you; they are His purpose for your life on this earth, and all you have to do is make those desires a reality. In all that you go through, there is a pot at the end of the rainbow which is Jesus. This book is very simple; it's not meant to impress you but to lend a hand as you walk out your process. There is no reason to be ashamed about where your path is taking you in this season of your life. It's real, and going through a process happens to all of us. We each may experience different circumstances but the outcome, if you know Jesus, is that you win!

I pray that as you read this book, you will hear the voice of God clearly, and every word you begin to speak from this day forward will become anointed words to create change in your life as well as those around you.

May Father God reward you at the appointed time because you have fought the good fight of faith and you have stood every test and trial that came your way and endured until the end. Through all the hurt and pain, you still showed love. May Father God call you his fervent, faithful servant! In Jesus' Name, Amen.

Broken Beyond Pieces

I come broken, tattered and torn

Take me, restore me, wash and cleanse me

Forgive me of my sins.

Remove ungodly thoughts, remove all the pain

Make me Lord, please make me whole again.

Show me how to birth what's in me out of me.

For Your Glory, Your kingdom, oh Lord, use me.

I am nothing without you

Can't do it on my own.

I give my life to you, oh Lord

Give me a brand new song.

Ashamed to tell my story

Ashamed to let hurt show.

But Father God you see me

And you're the only one who knows.

Episode I: What???

What do you do when you find out that your spouse is having an affair? Most people go *berserk*! For a moment (or a week) you may even lose your mind! Oh yeah, you might fantasize about cutting his thing right off! Or maybe it should just fall off for being in the wrong place! You just might plan his next meal with a little sprinkle of arsenic, or even his funeral! Or how about putting a tracking device on his car? Yep, let's see where he goes, and, oh yeah, we can't omit what you will do to the prostitute he's sleeping with! Yes, I said *prostitute*, because she's not married to him and certainly time and money are being spent. Whew! Okay, I'll calm down.... My goodness, they're just thoughts, right?

For a minute when you find out what your spouse is doing, and the flesh takes over and you are about to go bonkers, STOP! THINK, LOOK, and LISTEN and BREATHE! Satan, the devil, our adversary, wants to have control of your mind, your every thought and emotion, but DON'T LET HIM DO IT! Instead, **BREATHE and PRAY,** and begin to ask God to help you. Begin to remind yourself that *greater is He (God) that is in me (you) than he that is in the world.* Begin to take your every thought captive to the obedience of Christ. Remember, you are in Christ. **If Christ is not in you, now would be a good time to find Him.** Say this prayer from your heart and out loud: *Dear Lord Jesus, come into my heart. Forgive me of my sin. Wash me and cleanse me. Set me free. Jesus, thank you that you died for me. I believe that you have risen from the dead and that you are coming back again for me. Fill me with your Holy*

Spirit and Fire. Give me a passion for the lost and a hunger for the things of God and a Holy boldness to preach the gospel of Jesus Christ. I'm saved, I'm born again, I'm forgiven, and I'm on my way to Heaven because I have Jesus in my heart. **Now breathe and count....** 10, 9, 8, 7... ..oh yes, it could all seem to be falling down around you, but God *is*! ... 6, 5, 4... Oh yes, you could make that man pay for the pain he has made you feel..., but God *is*! ... 3, 2, 1. Whew! Thank you Jesus!

At that very moment, you just made a choice not to allow anger and rage to have control over your actions. But you know what? Not everyone is blessed to have Jesus Christ in them and allow Him to work out their issues, and that is why so many people end up in domestic violence or even *dead*! Nothing was in them to snap their mind back.

It's okay to get angry; it's a natural reaction, but don't follow through with your anger and commit a crime. It's no joke to discover that your husband is being unfaithful. Right about now, you may hate him, and you probably hate the other woman. You may hate yourself and question your own worth and value. So many feelings are going on inside you that you feel like you are about to explode.

You probably also want to know who else knows about the infidelity. Do his co-workers know? Do my friends know? How about his family? What are they saying about me? What are my spouse and the other woman saying about me? How long have I been a fool?

Then once you find out the answers to the questions, you want to drive by when you suspect they're together so you can see. All kind of things go through your mind, and it's okay as long as you regain control over your mind and don't turn your fantasies into ruinous action. It's terrible, but it happens, and the pain is real. You pray, cry and cry, scream, kick, pray, and cry some more. You may try to find a friend to talk to but find no one, or if you do, they have no advice for you, or the advice they have seems crazy, so you feel even more alone. You're trying to make sense of a dreadful situation.

Eventually, when you do calm down, your brain just becomes numb, and now you can't think at all. Then feelings of hurt, betrayal, and worthlessness begin to overtake you, and you may feel as though someone just took a knife, cut your heart out, and is squeezing it until it is lifeless.

Whew! You think, this is a lot to deal with. And you may begin to obsess over questions like "What have I done so bad to make him cheat?" STOP! STOP! STOP! YOU DID NOTHING WRONG!

A person is unfaithful because *they* want to be. They made a choice, and there is something in *them,* not *you,* that needs to be dealt with. Jesus loves you. You are somebody and worthy to be loved as Christ loves the Church. God made you beautiful; he molded you in His hands. Jeremiah 29:11 lets you know that He has a plan and purpose for your life; trust Him to walk with you through your process.

The Bible tells us in Hebrews 13:4, "M*arriage is honorable among all, and the bed undefiled; but fornicators and adulterers God will judge."* There is no reason whatsoever for a person to be unfaithful in a marriage. Yes, I know it happens all the time, and yes, I know society and the media glorify it, but the word of God says *no*, it is not okay! Marriage is based on covenant, and when two people marry, God stands as a witness to the marriage, sealing it with a covenant of faithfulness and enduring commitment. And when a spouse is unfaithful, that covenant is broken.

As we look at unfaithfulness, remember that it encompasses more than the spouse having sex outside of marriage. There are lies, abandonment, hiding, deception and manipulation of family members and friends. There is a home that you built together where special gatherings of family and friends took place. Now that home is no longer a place of warmth and happiness. As I stated in the beginning, infidelity infects everyone around you. Friends and families are having to choose sides, children if any, are being pulled in different directions.

If you are in the church, "church folks" begin to judge you and your spouse and talk behind your back. I said "church folks" because these are not the true Christians, and their behavior at times like this is what betrays them. "Church folks" are the ones who show up unfailingly on Sunday, sit in the pews, whisper, and criticize the service, the people and everything that happens. They go to Bible study and prayer service, and shout, speak in tongues and fall out on the floor. They may have their cliques, but they bear no fruit and save no souls. I expect you have met these "church folks."

On the other hand, a Christian will come to you in love and ask if there is anything they can do for you and your husband. They will pray with you and encourage you, and they won't gossip about your situation. A Christian will have genuine concern for you and your husband and have your best interest at heart.

Emotions, The Game Called "Life"

It's hard to know when to fold them
It's hard to know when to hold them
You roll the dice once
You roll the dice twice
It's all a gamble
called the game of life
Sometimes you may lose
Sometimes you may win
So you roll the dice again and again
It's a chance you take
No matter how big or small
One thing is bound to happen
You will take a fall
It's up to you on how you get up
Hold on real tight
The game of life is a bit rough
You might find yourself
On the rugged mountain side
You might find yourself
On top and feeling high
Once you think you've got it
Not a worry in sight
Something comes along
And knocks you into the night.
It's hard to understand what is going on
Although the rules are written
Things seem so far beyond.

That's the way it is in this game called life
You continue to roll the dice
Until the end of time.

II: Now That I know, What Should I Do?

After going through all the emotions, it's crucial that you understand the difference between the angry feelings that you have and the self-destructive behaviors that might grow out of those feelings if you don't find a way to deal with them.

At this stage your brain really needs to seek Godly counsel, a helping friend, someone who can think a bit clearer. At this point it's time to rethink your marriage. Ask yourself these questions: Are you still committed to it? Is there any hope for restoring your marriage? Should you confront your spouse with what you know? A lot of times when the husband is confronted, he becomes angry, because he has to own up to his selfish ways. The truth is out: no longer is he "Casanova", but an adulterous, lying, cheating whoremonger, a selfish individual lacking in self control. How dare he become angry at you! But it happens. What you have to remember is that it's not your husband but a wrong spirit operating within him. What you must know is that God is a restorer and He can restore your marriage, but it takes both your husband and you working together as one. **So now, my sister, walk in stride with God. He and you are in control!**

Stride one: Confront your husband. Do not put up with his affair one more second. Often when a person is a Christian, they think that they have to put up with such foolishness, but please hear this: the minute your spouse decided to have sex outside the marriage or to abuse you and not love you as Christ loves the Church, he broke covenant to God and to you. He allowed unclean spirits to come and dwell inside of him. The word says *what God has joined together let no man put asunder*. If your spouse does not listen, do not argue with him, but just try to refrain from knocking his stupid head off! Hey, just *keeping it real*! Now move to…

Stride two: Take one or two persons whom you trust and talk to him again, and if he still does not listen and continues in his selfish ways stroll on to....

Stride three: Go to your church leader, if you are connected to a church. If not, find someone with spiritual authority whom you trust to confide in. If your spouse continues to carry on with this behavior, then run to....

Stride four: Cut him off! Have no more conversations, no more inclusion in family functions, no more sex with the snake--cut him slap off! (I'm not saying your husband is a snake; it's the spirit within him.) The picture I'm painting is that your spouse has failed to fulfill his biblical role as loving husband, leader of the home and servant of God. He is living in sin. You don't submit to sin. The word of God says to flee and resist it. Matthew 18:15-17 says:

> *Moreover, if your brother sins against you, go and tell him his fault between you and him alone. If he hears you, you have gained your brother. But if he will not hear, take with you one or two more, that by the mouth of two or three witnesses every word may be established. And if he refuses to hear them, tell it to the church. But if he refuses even to hear the church, let him be to you like a heathen and a tax collector.*

Yes, I know the church says to love, and the church says love covers a multitude of sin, but the church has gone too far and become soft on sin. That's why so much sin goes on in the church and why many affairs occur among so-called Preachers and Christians. To cover a multitude of sin does not mean to overlook it; it means to go to your brother in love and talk to him. It means not to gossip about his sins to others. It means to work it out, be delivered from the sin, let it go, and do that thing no longer!

Keeping It Real: When Infidelity Strikes

Jesus loves us, but He does not put up with our sin at all! When we continue to sin, Jesus cuts us off! Our prayers are hindered (1st Peter 3:7; Ephesians 4:31-32; and James 1:5-7). Jesus does not hear our prayers until we confess, repent and turn from our wicked ways. Forgive my harshness, but I'm just *keeping it real*. Give your husband a taste of what it will be like without you, and maybe, just maybe, he will see the light.

The truth is that when it comes to you and your marriage, the only help you are going to get is by going to the throne of God, and seeking His face and His direction for your situation. People really do not have the answers. A lot of times they will not stand for what is right. Most of the time they have issues too. Some people don't really care about what you are going through, and others just don't know how to help you.

The Silence of God

The silence of God does not mean
He is not listening
The silence of God does not mean
He has not heard your prayers.
The silence of God does not mean
He has abandoned you
The silence of God does not mean
He does not care
Contrary;
The silence of God means
He is in the process of shifting
and moving things in the heavens
for your earthly good.
The silence of God means
He has already met your every need.
The silence of God means
He loves you and knows
what you are going through.
The silence of God means
He has lifted every burden
and worked all things out just for you.
The silence of God means.....
when He speaks you will know!

Episode III: My Journey (Personal Testimony)

As I share with you my journey, first of all know that I am in no way bashing my ex-spouse. This is my testimony, and he just happened to be a part of it. I have no bitterness or unforgiveness in my heart. As a matter of fact, he and I communicate very well. Just because the marriage did not work does not make my ex-spouse or myself a bad person. In life some things just are, and some things just happen....

In my situation I had to totally 700% trust Holy Spirit to lead and guide my every thought and footstep. I chose the number 700 because 7 is the number of completion in the Spirit which will manifest itself in the physical. I had to make sure I was in God's presence night and day so that I could hear his voice. My prayer was for God to *fix my marriage or move me*. Those words became a part of my everyday vocabulary. There came a time when I thought I would snap! But then, God… 10, 9, 8, 7, yes, kept my mind in perfect peace. This was serious; this was my life! Do or die! No, I was not in an emergency room fighting to stay alive. I was alive physically, but death was coming to me mentally and emotionally, and this eventually would have destroyed me physically.

The enemy was trying to steal my mind, my identity, and the calling God has placed within me. In my case, I had to move to live! I had to give up to live! At some point in the process (and most of us are taught that this is "selfish"), but there comes a time when it *is* all about you! You have to fight the enemy, just as Jesus did when He was in the wilderness (Mark 1:13). The word of God says, "*We wrestle not against flesh and blood but against principalities, against powers, against the rulers of the darkness of this age, against a spiritual host of wickedness in the heavenly places*" (Ephesians 6:12).

What I realized was that in my process, God was perfecting me! He was molding, shaping and drawing me closer to Him. He was showing me my imperfections so He could position me for His glory. Even with an unfaithful spouse, God was still showing me what was inside of me, good and bad. He was moving and shifting me.

Sometimes our circumstances have to change, and the process of change can be very painful. What I learned is that no matter what we go through, it is still about what's inside of us which God is shaping, and it's all for His glory. I would have loved for my marriage to work. No one enters into a marriage to have it broken and shattered into pieces, but marriage takes two people willing to work together, willing to respect, trust and communicate with each other. Sexual intimacy is for the spouse and the spouse alone!

Okay, I suppose inquiring minds want to know. I'll give you a brief summary of what happened to me. I was fed up! I plead with God to remove me before I snapped. Things had progressed to the final stage. For years I lived with my X spouse lustfulness, affairs, pornography, strip clubs, massage parlors, cybersex, hotels, disrespect toward me… in short, his sinful life! There, I said it! Yeah, "for real" I went through all of that. I'm still alive and so is he, praise The Almighty God!

I ask myself why I put up with that type of behavior for so long. Only The Lord knows. But I think what happens is that some of us women stay for the sake of our children. Some of us stay because there is fear of not being able to connect with anyone else. We stay because we think that we are the problem, and we deserve to be treated as such. We all stay for different reasons. But I truly believe that most of us stay because we give ourselves fully to our spouse, and somewhere in our mind we think that they will change or that we can make them change.

Keeping It Real: When Infidelity Strikes

In reality, only God can change the heart of a person. And people do what they want to do because they want to. It's a choice. We are not responsible for another person's actions, but we *are* responsible for our reactions.

Here was my reaction: I was sitting in the Wal-Mart parking lot with tears streaming from my eyes, trying to get myself together to go into the store. I was blowing my nose, and carrying on terribly, my eyes puffed up and red, the whole dramatic act. We've all been there, and some of us are still there. (*Just keeping it real!*)

At that moment, Holy Spirit laid it upon my heart to call this contractor that I knew who had just finished remodeling an apartment complex. Holy Spirit said to me, when he answers the phone tell him that you have an issue and need a place to stay. With all of my pride along with embarrassment, and I do mean all of it--I did not want to do this—and yet because of my extreme desperation, I obeyed The Holy Spirit.

Now, as I was dialing the number, I said to Holy Spirit, "Okay, now, God, if this is you, then you are going to have to make a way for me to pay rent that is affordable." So, as the man picked up the phone, I said, "Hello this is Christine. I was on your property yesterday, and it looks really nice. "Thank you," he said. I went on, "I have an issue and need a place to stay." He said, "Well, okay, go by the property and tell the manager to let you look at some apartments--whatever you want--1, 2, 3 bedrooms." I said, "Okay, thank you so much." Then just when I got ready to ask him how much the rent would be, he added, "Better yet, let me call my wife and let her know that I'm going to let you move on the property rent free. I don't have to know your issue, and you can stay as long as you like."

Wow! With tears in my eyes, I blubbered, "You would do that for me?" He said, "Yes, you've helped me a lot over the years, so yeah, go pick your apartment."

What a relief! To make a long story short--and not *all* about me, let's just say that I picked out the apartment. Then God told me, "Take nothing but your personal belongings and articles for ministry." Now I'm thinking, "Father God this is crazy, but I'll do it."

So I began moving things little by little in my vehicle. On my way to work, I would go by the apartment and drop items off. Now mind you, my spouse was still doing his thing and paying me no attention. The day that I moved my last item into the apartment, just as it hit the floor, I heard the voice of God say, "Now, go back!" "WHAT? God, is this you?" And He said in a still, small voice, "Go back. You have proven to be a fervent, faithful servant who will pick up your cross and follow me at all cost." I could not believe it. I sat on the floor and cried like a baby. I cried because I was so touched that God called me His faithful servant. Then I cried harder because He was sending me back. "Really God?"

What I've come to realize is that when you are walking through your process, you may cry a lot! But you know what? God is not moved by our tears. What moves Him is our faithful obedience and relationship to Him.

I know it was God who spoke to me because I know his voice. His word says *My sheep hear My voice and I know them, and they follow Me* (John 10:27). So I began to slowly return back to something worse than a hell hole, as I called it, while saying to God, "Well, if you are sending me back, that means things are going to be better. It means you have restored my marriage." WRONG! Things only got worse.

Keeping It Real: When Infidelity Strikes

As a matter of fact, there was a period of silence where it felt as though God had left me.

My spouse and I were sleeping in separate rooms--no conversation, nothing moving, nothing shaking, *nada*! And it was terrible. There came a point where I had absolutely no one to confide in, no phone calls, and no face to face human communication.

After much, much heart ache, spiritual warfare, and prayer, God released me. One Saturday morning after not hearing the voice of God for almost two months after returning home, God spoke to me in a gentle voice: "I'm releasing you, My daughter; you can take anything you want from here. The first time I told you to take nothing but personal items and things for ministry because I was sending you back. I sent you back to give him a second chance and to test your obedience. You have proven that you will stand even in adversity, and he has proven he is not ready to change. Know that I am God. Know that I am He who sets man free. Sometimes, or should I say some people, need to be shaken because they are so bound. All I do is provide the shaking; it's up to the person to make a choice. In your case, the man in your house will not hear. He is operating in such disobedience that his ears are shut and his eyes are closed. The enemy has him trapped, and he does not want to be free. The husband you once knew is no longer there." God continued to speak to me and told me to know that *that day* was the beginning of a new day, and He released me to go in peace, in the name of Jesus.

With tears flowing down my face, I realized that God really does hear our prayers, and He does answer and He never leaves us; nor will He ever forsake us. I also realized that we have a choice. It was the choice of my spouse to continue to have his affairs and sexual sins. My choice was not to live in an unfaithful marriage or infected environment any more.

Because God's word says marriage is honorable and the bed undefiled, He had to answer my prayer. Remember my prayer was, "Father God, fix my marriage or move me."

So I packed up my things thinking I would go back to the apartment complex where God had given me favor, rent free. WRONG. The first apartment I thought I was moving into had a bug problem. The second one also had a bug problem, which was strange for a newly remodeled building. And the third one the manager on duty had rented to someone else.

It was at that point that I realized provision for that place was only for the moment of the first test that God had put before me. I told the owner of the property, "Thank you for everything, but I don't think God wants me to live here." He was very nice and said anytime he could help me to let him know.

Meanwhile, back at the hell hole, I packed, looked for an apartment and waited for God to show me where He wanted me to move. In the process I became frustrated.

I was driving around and had looked at several apartments where I thought Holy Spirit was telling me to go. Nothing was working out. The first apartment had burned, the second one had too many buildings. The third one wanted too much personal information, and the fourth one was too expensive. About that time, God and I were having a serious conversation, and it was not a happy one. I was screaming from the depth of my soul to God, "WHERE DO YOU WANT ME TO LIVE? WHERE DO YOU WANT ME TO GO?" Then I heard a soft voice say, "Go there." I was passing a fifth apartment complex, a very nice gated community. I asked God, "There?" thinking I could not afford it (oh ye of little faith). He said yes, so I responded, "Okay, God."

Keeping It Real: When Infidelity Strikes

When I arrived to speak with the manager, God showed favor, and planted me in that community. The number 5 represents God's grace, and that apartment was the fifth one I had looked at that day. You see, when you have a relationship with God, you can talk to him in that tone of voice and be real with Him, and He can be real with you, and He will come through.

God will lead and guide you through your entire process, and the outcome will be His choice for your life. As long as you are keeping yourself connected to Him and your heart pure, and you are walking in obedience to Him, He will answer your prayers and help you. He will lift your heavy burden. He will put love, peace and immeasurable joy in your heart. Holy Spirit will lead you to where He wants you to be and provide provision for your journey. Don't be moved by your own emotions. Trust God, not man. Hear God, not man. Be moved by God, not man. Let Holy Spirit tell you when, where, and how, and then be obedient. Know that God's grace is sufficient!

I need to say this to those women whom God has called into ministry: In spite of what you are going through with your spouse, you must still preach God's word. In spite of what you are going through in life, God has commissioned you to preach His word, in season and out of season (2nd Timothy 4: 1-5).

At one point I thought that I should step down as minister of the church where I worship because I did not want to cause harm to the people of God. I went to my Pastor and told him I would step down out of the pulpit. My Pastor being who he is, said to me, "No, you're okay. I know you, and if anyone says anything to you tell them to come see me."

One thing I know to be true is that if you are called to preach God's word, there is no way you can lay it down. And God will move, shift and position you to do His work. You have to continue on the battlefield for the Lord.

Whatever you walk through in your marriage or in any part of your life, it is all for the Glory of God. So hold your head up in spite of it all; keep yourself pure before God; preach His word and save souls. Put your marriage at the feet of Jesus.

When you are faithful and obedient to God, He will take care of all your needs. God's purpose for your life will be fulfilled. I am a walking, living, speaking, writing testimony as to what God will do.

Keeping It Real: When Infidelity Strikes

Shhhhhhhhhh

It looks picture perfect but only God really knows

What goes on between two people behind closed doors.

If walls and carpet could talk I wonder what they would say?

How can two people who are in love carry on that way?

Shhhhhhhhh don't say a word or your life may come to an end.

Look there's no one here where are all your friends?

It looks picture perfect but only God really knows

What goes on between two people behind closed doors.

Episode IV: Shhhhhhh It's a Secret

After walking out my own journey, I realized how many women are hurting. God began to place women in my path to minister to. Why? Because I have walked where they are walking. I've learned that whatever we go through in life is a lesson for us personally. And whatever we learn is to be shared with someone else who may be experiencing something similar. Most importantly, God gets all the glory when we share and help someone else.

We all think that we would know if we were being abused by someone we love. But the truth is that most of us women never acknowledge to ourselves or others that our husband is hurting us. Sometimes abuse just becomes a part of our everyday life. The truth is that most women don't want anyone to know the pain in their heart so they camouflage it.

Some of us go to church on Sundays, smile, and have a few emotional movements in what we call the "spirit of God," only to go home hurt and broken. Some of us party, drink, use drugs, or sleep around to try and make the hurt go away. Some wear clothing to cover up bruises or use other strategies to hide the abuse by our husbands. Why? Because we live in a society where the world says anything and everything goes in a relationship, and the church preaches that you cannot divorce your spouse unless he commits adultery. You are taught to stay with him and forgive because God forgives you for your sins. Hog wash!

Keeping It Real: When Infidelity Strikes

So he beats you and kicks you, and the church says to stay, forgive, and love him in spite of it. He sexually abuses you, and the church says your body is not your own; you are to submit to your husband. He sleeps around and puts you at risk of venereal disease, and the church advises you to seek counseling. That's crazy! I'm not saying counseling is wrong. It's only wrong if nothing is changing. You should never be in a relationship with someone who does not appreciate and respect the awesome, beautifully created woman of God that you are.

Being unfaithful is not always sexual. There are many other types of unfaithfulness, and it happens in all walks of life regardless of social status, age, gender or color. It's very painful to think of your own spouse, someone you love, as an abusive, disrespectful person. Sure, he may be very loving, caring, great in bed, and charming much of the time. Maybe he is great with the children, and maybe your friends and family adore him. But they don't see what goes on behind closed doors.

Perhaps your spouse says he doesn't intend to hurt you, and maybe he genuinely does feel sorry later. He may have many wonderful qualities and you may be thankful for many of the things he does for you, but none of that can excuse actions, words or threats which hurt you or the children or which make you feel unsafe, shameful, or worthless.

Sometimes your spouse may try to convince you that he is doing this because he loves you. Don't fall for his foolish talk. Even though it's supposed to be "love," it is not. Love never involves abuse of any kind.

Something else you should know: Your spouse is not the only one that can abuse you. Anyone can abuse you: parents, siblings, aunts, uncles, teachers, grandparents, colleagues, or even a best friend. Abuse is an unjust practice and comes in many forms. It can be invisible but over time can begin to take a physical toll. Living with an abusive spouse will begin to make you more bitter each day, and you will begin to lose who God created you to be in the process.

Getting help when you're in an abusive relationship always involves reaching out to someone. **Don't keep it a secret.** Tell someone about your situation, no matter how embarrassing or painful it may be, and let people help you sort through it.

When going through a process, you must have some form of release that is healthy. My release was God! Thank you, Jesus. Then towards the end of my process, God put a person in my life with whom I went to Bible College who helped me get through the rest of my journey. We became prayer warriors, friends, and sisters. She was going through a similar situation, and we helped each other walk through our process. Now she is my best sister and friend ever. God has blessed her with the love of her life and she is moving forward.

One thing you must realize is that the enemy, satan will always try to keep you quiet. If he can keep you quiet, then he can't be exposed for his actions, and he can keep you in bondage. I'm not saying that your spouse is satan, but that his *actions* are of the enemy. Jesus spoke to Peter in Matthew 16:23 and said, *"Get behind Me, satan! You are an offense to Me, for you are not mindful of the things of God, but the things of men.* Satan will use feelings of shame and guilt, so his lies will not be uncovered. I'm not saying for you to tell the street committee your business but instead to seek Godly counsel and pray that God will connect you to a trustworthy prayer warrior, friend or sister to help you through your journey.

"Typical Man"

You tell me that you love me, I wonder if it's true.

Although I feel it in my heart when I make love to you.

You say you enjoy the married life but what do you do?

Go and hang out in bars for singles and not two.

I say it does not annoy me but in my eyes you can see.

When you walk out that door a hasty change comes over me.

I know sometimes one needs space.

But I'm afraid someone will take my place.

Don't mean to sound selfish don't mean to sound cruel.

But I have dedicated my whole life to loving only you.

As time goes on maybe I'll understand you really do love me?

And going out is just typical of a man?

Episode V: "Typical Man" Not Accepted

We are often told that a man is going to cheat. We are told that abuse in the form of cheating is the behavior of typical men. No! No! No! The various types of abuse in relationships include neglect, physical abuse, sexual abuse, verbal abuse, and emotional abuse--and none of this is acceptable. I personally have added Pornography, Cybersex, Strip Clubs, and Massage Parlors to the abuse list. I repeat, none of this is typical or acceptable!

Neglect: This is the most common type of abuse. It entails treating someone or something carelessly or not paying them proper attention or looking after their needs. When you are the victim, you hurt all the time because you feel alone and abandoned. Your spouse is no longer your friend. He goes out without you, hangs out with his friends and doesn't invite you along. The only time he pays attention to you is when he wants sex. He is not there for you when you need him the most. When he hurts your feelings, he doesn't apologize. He lives his life as if you weren't married and rarely considers you. He does his thing and you do yours. He doesn't show any interest in you or what you do. You can rarely reach him by phone, and he comes home late. Neglect can also be when your spouse is spending time, talking and laughing with another woman in the same way he would normally do with you. When you begin to suspect that you are no longer exciting enough, you then feel unloved, disrespected and alone.

Verbal abuse: Because this type of abuse is "only" words, many people don't view it as abuse until there is an emotional breakdown. Negative name calling, like labeling you "stupid" or "idiot," is your spouse's way of destroying your self-esteem. The blame game is another form of verbal abuse.

Your spouse blames you for everything wrong so he looks like the good guy. He may threaten to leave if you don't do what he says. He may humiliate you in front of friends and family, including calling you names, putting you down, insulting you, yelling at you, laughing at you, or making jokes that are personal.

Sexual abuse: This is any form of touching or intercourse against your will. Exploitation of your body may also include taking pictures of you for sexual purposes, asking you to watch sexual videos, asking you to touch someone else's private parts, and making sexual references to your body. Being forced to touch or have sex with your spouse or someone else against your will is sexual abuse. An abusive love relationship can make you feel very ashamed.

Physical abuse: This can be the easiest abuse for others to spot because the clues are obvious when someone hits, slaps, beats, burns, kicks, or stabs you. However, there may not be evidence when someone grabs your arm, shakes you, or pushes you around, but these are also definitely forms of physical abuse.

Emotional/Mental abuse: Emotional abuse is the most difficult to recognize. It includes calling you names, putting you down, insulting you, and breaking your possessions. Control is a huge part of emotional abuse and involves chronic anger, jealousy, accusations, and distrust, as well as more subtle tactics such as intimidation and manipulation. This type of abuse is the hardest to spot because the injuries aren't physical or immediately visible. Emotional abuse can be mistaken for passionate or intense love and can lead you to believe that you are unworthy of any other type of love, care and support. You remain with the abusive spouse, believing that no other person would desire a relationship with you.

Pornography, Cybersex, Strip Clubs, Massage Parlors: These practices are not only abusive to you, but to your spouse; as he participates in such activities, he is abusing himself. This is an area that is sweeping the world as well as the Christian community and destroying marriages. Yet pastors rarely preach or talk about it from the pulpit because if the truth were really told, many of them are guilty of indulging in such activities themselves. Allow me to take you on a tour of these practices.

Pornography is a closet addiction which grabs a person in a moment of weakness and holds them in its clutches. Planting seeds of isolation, it attacks and destroys relationships and robs a person of his self-respect. Pornography holds a person in bondage as he loses himself in a fantasy world. I can witness first hand as to the demonic stronghold that this type of sexual sin can have on your spouse.

It can begin with your spouse viewing something that appears harmless, such as airbrushed photos in a magazine or a click on the internet, and bam! There it is, and he's hooked. Soon his desire for more graphic material becomes intense and more frequent. He can't break away from it and may tell you there's nothing wrong with learning new things to enhance intimacy between the two of you. Suddenly you become his pleasure-giving machine, and you are being compared to the images he has entangled his mind in. You are no longer enough to please him, and soon neither are the images. So he moves on to the next stages: cybersex, strip clubs, massage parlors, and woman after woman. You have now become replaced.

Cybersex is also called computer sex or Internet sex and is a virtual sex encounter in which your spouse and one or more persons connected remotely via computer network send each other sexually explicit messages describing a sexual experience. It is a form of sexual role play in which he pretends he is having actual sex. In one form, this fantasy sex is accomplished by his describing his actions and responding to those of his chat partner in a mostly written form designed to stimulate their own sexual feelings and fantasies.

Cybersex sometimes includes real-life masturbation. Your spouse can have this kind of sex within existing or intimate relationships, with lovers who are geographically distant, or with several individuals who have no prior knowledge of one another and who meet him in virtual spaces or cyberspaces and may even remain anonymous to one another. With webcams and Skype anything is possible. Usually if your spouse is involved in such on-line activities and you walk into the room, he will hurry up and try to pull up another screen. I remember I had a web-cam to keep in touch with family members who were abroad, but I was not comfortable with my spouse having one. Still, he managed to do his stuff anyway. I said that, to say this. You cannot stop a person from doing what they want to do. Eventually cybersex is not enough, and he wants more and more so the next stage becomes:

Strip clubs: An adult entertainment venue in which striptease or other erotic sex acts are regularly performed. Strip clubs typically adopt a nightclub or bar style, but can also adopt a cabaret style. After the shows or as the shows are going on, women often give men special lap dances, or men pay to have sex with these women. (It's amazing to me how these places can be advertised on big billboard signs, but we rarely see anything of Jesus Christ on big billboards.) At this point, your spouse is totally lust-driven. He may take the women to hotels or even to your home.

Massage parlors are your spouse's next stop. These are businesses where customers can receive a massage. The term "massage" may be used as a cover for paid sexual favors and is just another form of prostitution. This adds a little more privacy; in other words, it's more hidden than if he was at a strip club. Massage parlors are everywhere throughout this country and are often simply brothels in disguise.

If your spouse is involved in any of this, it is not good for him or you. You are at risk of venereal disease and even violent encounters with other women with whom he is involved or their partners. Trust me; I know because I have walked every single one of these paths. Praise God that He kept my body free from any type of disease.

Let me share with you something that I had to come to terms with while in my own journey. Until your spouse acknowledges he has a problem and makes a choice to seek help, there can be no deliverance, and your marriage will be on a constant roller coaster. The enemy, the devil, our adversary, has full rein in your husband's life. You cannot make a person do something they do not want to do. You can pray, talk, go on a fast, do battle in the heavens, but until your husband decides he has had enough and seeks help and transforms his way of thinking, there is nothing you can do.

Your pain is deep because now you are having to deal with your own self-image, your own what-ifs, your own thoughts of "maybe I'm too fat, not good enough in the bed, not pretty enough... What have I done?" and the list goes on. *STOP!* Don't let your mind go there, everything God made is good and very good, and *God made you. Stop blaming yourself for your spouse's behavior.*

Neither abuse nor sexual sins are a source of lasting satisfaction. Your spouse who is entangled in such activities is looking to fill a deeper need in his life. Often, there is a generational reason for your spouse's behavior, but this is a topic which would fill another book. Whatever the case, having a true relationship with God is the only way that your spouse can be free. You cannot fill that void.

Intimacy means being known inside and out and being loved for who you are. Because we were designed for relationships, God made us with a desire for intimacy. Being known inside out is scary to some people because it entails vulnerability, so they go searching for intimacy in less threatening places such as pornography, cybersex, strip clubs, massage parlors and affairs, all of which only bring temporary satisfaction. Your spouse may hit or verbally abuse you because he longs for that power and authority to rule and the filling of that hole inside of him that only God can give to him.

If you are living in this type of environment, I can't stress enough that your marriage is in deep need of help. Your spouse is not himself, and he has now opened the door for all types of ungodly spirits to enter into your space. I remember God used to refer to my ex-spouse as "the man in your house. Then he took me to Isaiah 54:5, which reads: *"For your maker is your husbandman. The Lord of hosts is His name; And your Redeemer is the Holy One of Israel."* God was showing me that my spouse was not my husband anymore because of the way he was treating me, and to turn instead to God to be my husbandman. The same holds true for you. The man in your house is not your husband right now.

Godly Love

I shall abide in the shadow of thy wings

In the shadows of thy wings you rescue me.

A mere moment I had forsaken you

But with great mercies you covered me

Now I can truly say my heart belongs to you

Soul ties broken I am brand new.

Deep in my mind were unclean thoughts

You washed them all away and made me see

For You are everything man can't satisfy

Abide in me and I in You.

Never again will I turn the other way.

You picked me up and saved my day

I shall abide in the shadows of thy wings

In the shadow of thy wings You love me

Soul Ties

Everyone your spouse is sleeping with is now in your bed. Some of the things he does or says to you are now intertwined with the things he may have said or done with other women. The term used is "soul ties." Remember the word of God says that the two become one when married, one flesh, so think about this: your husband becomes one with everyone that he sleeps with. They have joined themselves together sexually. That person's soul is now entangled with your spouse's, and soul ties must be broken.

So now, as if you didn't have enough to deal with already, you may be asking what in the world is a soul tie? Sorry, just *keeping it real*. A soul tie is the knitting together of two souls that can either bring tremendous blessings in a Godly relationship or tremendous destruction when made with the wrong person.

Soul ties can be sexual. Soul ties can also develop between any two people who are open to one another. For example, you can become soul tied to family, friends, co-workers and the leadership you are under. The unity we have with others is an open expression of our soul ties. The strength of those soul ties depends upon how deeply involved with another our heart becomes; therefore, we need to carefully examine our friends, male and female, before it becomes a covenant or relationship, because people that come into our lives can influence the shaping of our lives and our walk with Jesus.

Keeping It Real: When Infidelity Strikes

2 Corinthians 6:14 says, *"Be ye not unequally yoked together with unbelievers; for what fellowship hath righteousness with unrighteousness? And what communion hath light with darkness?"* 2 Corinthians 6:17 adds: *"Wherefore come out from among them, and be ye separate, saith the Lord, and touch not the unclean thing; and I will receive you."*

When a person who is connected to another is governed by impure motives or the desire for selfish gain, the soul tie between them can make that selfish one manipulate and abuse the other. A person can actually control another through soul ties, because the minds of the two are open to one another. For example, have you ever noticed the cliques in the church or even at work? Usually one group has their pick and chooses whom they like and don't like. Then if a person in the clique decides they want to be a friend to someone that the people in the clique don't like, the people in the clique become angry, and the other person will have to decide whether or not to befriend the outsider or stay in the clique. That's a negative kind of soul tie.

Another kind is a Godly soul tie, which can be described not only by the word *knit*, but also by the word *cleave*, which means to bring close together, follow close after, be attached to someone, or adhere to one another as with glue.

If we look at Godly friendship soul ties, we will see in 1 Samuel 18:1-3: *And it came to pass, when he had made an end of speaking unto Saul, that the **soul** of Jonathan was **knit** with the **soul** of David, and Jonathan loved him as his **own soul**. And Saul took him that day, and would not let him go home to his father's house anymore. Then Jonathan and David made a **covenant**, because he loved him as his own soul.*

The soul of Jonathan was knit with the soul of David, and Jonathan loved him as his own soul. This is simply a way of expressing Jonathan's total commitment and deep friendship with David. So you can see here, David and Jonathan actually formed a covenant because they loved each other so deeply. Their souls were knit together, tied or joined together as friends.

The stronger the bond or soul tie between friends, the deeper and more lasting the relationship is. The emotional and mental strengths of one sustain the other in times of adversity, difficulties or misfortune. The bond also allows them to rejoice with each other in the time of triumph.

When love between friends is pure and not polluted by selfish desire, the bond between them works well in their lives. Jesus also speaks of this kind of love in John 15:13: *"Greater love has no one than this, than to lay down one's life for his friends."* That is the kind of love Jonathan and David had, and that is why it was a Godly soul tie.

In order to have this kind of friendship, you have to be very selective and get wisdom from God. Let God establish your friends. Think about someone you consider to be your best friend. Now think about the relationship that you have with that person.

Ungodly Soul Ties

The Bible also warns against entering ungodly relationships. *"The righteous should choose his friends carefully, the way of the wicked leads them astray" (Proverbs 12:26).* This passage and others like it caution us against the wrong types of friends.

In ungodly relationships these soul ties may place us in emotional and mental bondage to others and cause us to do and say things to our own detriment. Romans 8:15 says: *"For ye have not received the spirit of bondage again to fear; but ye have received the Spirit of adoption, whereby we cry, Abba, Father."*

Ungodly soul ties can potentially be established if the relationship is not under the Lordship of Christ. God demands first place in our hearts; spouses are to be second, followed by children, family, friends and associates. When our strongest soul tie is to God, there is a divine covering and protection that will enable us to withstand forming ungodly soul ties. That divine covering is Holy Spirit.

God, the Father designed the universe to function with natural and spiritual laws that bring freedom to us when obeyed, but bondage and destruction when broken and violated. Just as two souls can be knit or made to cleave together in a covenant relationship, they can also be tied or knit together to form bondage and enslavement.

Sexual Soul Ties

We also have clear warning against fornication in Scripture. "The word of God says in I Corinthians 6:16- 18: *For this cause shall a man leave his father and mother, and shall be joined unto his wife, and the two shall be one flesh. Or do you not know and realize that when a man joins himself to a prostitute, he becomes one body with her? The two, it is written, shall become one flesh, but the person who is united to the Lord becomes one spirit with Him. Shun immorality and all sexual looseness; flee from impurity in thought, word, or deed. Any other sin which a man commits is one outside the body, but he who commits sexual immorality sins against his own body.*

Sexual involvement can form such entangling tentacles of soul ties that it is extremely hard to break off the relationship. I totally understand why sex outside of the marriage is forbidden. Because sex feels so good *(hey, just keeping it real),* it opens all kind of feelings and emotions. And those good feelings are just that--a good feeling for a moment. Now that person you just had sex with is in your mind 24/7, in your heart 24/7. You think about him daily. You smell his scent; oh yes, he is all in your spirit, mind and soul as if you are truly husband and wife. You can't sleep or eat if he doesn't call. Life as you used to know it takes a sudden turn, and you have become madly in lust. Yes, I said lust. You might call it love, but it's crazy lust.

Then there is a time factor. What is a time factor? All the times you spent together sexually, the places you went and so on.... at a certain time, day or night, or in a place when and where things used to happen, you automatically plug your mind set to that spot. For example, if at 9:00 pm he gave you a phone call, at 9:00 pm every night, you are looking for a call, and when it does not happen, you are frustrated. If you used to meet on Thursdays and have sex at a certain time, then on Thursdays at that particular time, you begin to fantasize about the experience.

Keeping It Real: When Infidelity Strikes

Think about it. Soul ties formed through illicit sexual involvement can be as strong and binding as those formed through the marriage covenant. Now imagine what happens when that person you are sleeping with does not ask you to marry him.

You actually go through all the symptoms and stages of a divorce not a good feeling. That's why soul ties formed in an ungodly manner must be broken, and a renewing of the mind must take place.

I can remember that things got to a point where just the touch of my ex-spouse made me cringe because he had become so entangled with sexual soul ties that I could feel them. Trust me when I say it's real. What I had to do was to keep myself constantly covered by the blood of Jesus. But if you are not connected spiritually to God, then you will not have a clue why you feel a certain way or why now being intimate with your spouse is so disgusting.

If your spouse is in a sexual relationship right now outside of marriage, he needs to STOP it now! No matter what kind of lies satan may put in your mind, don't agree with the enemy! For instance, satan may say, "It's okay for your husband to cheat. You know he loves you, and he will stop once he gets it out of his system." Or "keep praying; it's just a phase men go through."

NO! He needs to stop now! Do not listen to the lies of the enemy. You need to cover yourself with the blood of Jesus and ask God to remove any unclean spirits that may have attached themselves to you. Ask God to uncover all the tricks of the enemy and show you any open doors to your soul and spirit that need to be closed.

God does have a plan for you that's good. He's not anti-sex; in fact, sex was His idea in the first place. God created sex to be the deepest physical expression of intimacy between a man and woman. God is excited about sex, and He wants us to experience pure sexual fulfillment in the way that He planned. Unfortunately, some of us have taken it upon ourselves and allowed sexual sin to damage our sexuality, not to mention the mental and emotional parts of us.

God created sex and true intimacy to be expressed within marriage. If your marriage is to be restored, your mate must confess, be accountable, and transform his mind. The Bible tells us, *"If we confess our sins, God is faithful and just and will forgive us of our sins and purify us from all unrighteousness" (1 John 1:9).*

Confession means admitting that we've done wrong, agreeing with God that it is sin, and deciding to turn around and do the right thing from now on.

Accountability The temptations of sexual sin is greater when your spouse is alone, so for that reason, it is important for him to surround himself with Godly people who will build him up and support him in his efforts to be pure. If he is not willing to do that, then separate yourself from him. Accountability is the key to breaking the chains of sexual sin.

In my situation, my ex did not want to be accountable; he felt as though I was checking up on him and that if I trusted him, then he would not have to tell me what he did, or where he went or whom he talked to. Even when I explained to him that he gave me no reason to trust him, he still did not want to be accountable. If your marriage is going to be saved, accountability is a must.

Keeping It Real: When Infidelity Strikes

Transformation of the mind: Philippians 4:8 says, *"Finally, brothers, whatever is true, whatever is noble, whatever is right, whatever is pure, whatever is lovely, whatever is admirable — if anything is excellent or praiseworthy — think about such things."* A world saturated with sexual images has controlled your husband's thought life. He will be confronted with sexual images, and this will become his ongoing battleground.

The enemy will place lustful thoughts in his mind, and he will have relapses and remember images he has seen in the past. But he does not have to dwell on those thoughts. One thing he can do to reduce the temptation is to cut back on the number of "gateway images" he exposes himself to such as movies, magazines and bars. He must transform his mind.

Timothy 2:22 says, *"Flee the evil desires of youth, and pursue righteousness, faith, love and peace, along with those who call on the Lord out of a pure heart."* This includes working actively to replace sexual images in his mind with more wholesome thoughts.

If your spouse chooses not to do any of these things, then you must separate yourself from him... *"Love is patient, love is kind. It does not envy, it does not boast, it is not proud. It is not rude, it is not self-seeking, it is not easily angered, it keeps no record of wrongs. Love does not delight in evil but rejoices with the truth. It always protects, always trusts, always hopes, always perseveres"* (1 Corinthians 13: 4-7).

If your husband is not willing to replace the sexual sin images with positive ones, ask yourself this question, where is the love? He must be willing to invest time and renew his relationship with God and with you. If your husband is not willing to do that, then you have no choice but to put him at the feet of Jesus.

King David was known as "a man after God's own heart." But even David sinned sexually and got caught in the trap of his actions. He had an affair with Bathsheba and then had her husband killed to try to cover up his wrongdoing. However, once David was confronted with his sin, he was heartbroken. Psalm 51 demonstrates his anguish and shows how he opened his heart before God and pleaded for God to have mercy upon him, to forgive him and to create in him a clean heart. He asked God to purge him with hyssop. He was so broken that he wanted God to blot out all his iniquities (see 2 Samuel 11-12.)

No matter how dirty, broken and worthless your husband may feel, or what he has done, God can and will restore his purity and can renew your marriage. Tell your husband that he needs to say the prayer in this book and take the steps of confession, repentance and accountability. The Apostle Peter addresses the husbands and punctuates his address with the same gravity as Isaiah. In 1 Peter 3:7 he writes, *"Likewise, ye husbands, dwell with them according to knowledge, giving honor unto the wife, as unto the weaker vessel, and as being heirs together of the grace of life; that your prayers be not hindered."*

Your husband is to dwell with you "according to knowledge" or knowledgeably because we as women are referred to by God as the weaker vessel. You are a fellow-heir of the grace of life. In other wards a man may treat his wife harshly, more like a male slave than a wife, placing on her heavy physical loads she was not created to bear. The opposite of "knowledgeably" would be "insensitively" or "ignorantly." Peter calls on husbands to be considerate of their wives noting their physical frailty and taking excessive burdens from them. Husbands commit sin when they do not treat their wives respectfully. *"Behold, the Lord's hand is not shortened, that it cannot save; neither His ear heavy, that it cannot hear; but your iniquities have separated between you and your God, and your sins have hid his face from you, that He will not hear"* (Isaiah 59:1-2). There are so many places where the Bible shows us examples of what honor is by showing us dishonor. For example, we are commanded to honor to honor our father and mother, but how to do that is given to us by telling us things not to do (Exodus: 20:12 and Ephesians:1-3).

Peter cautions husbands to show great care in how they treat their wives. A man's spiritual well-being is in trouble if he does not honor, cherish, and protect his wife.

Prayer for your husband to say:

Father God, in Jesus' name, I humbly ask you to forgive me and cleanse me of the sins of adultery, and lust, abandonment, and abuse. I acknowledge it as sin and ask you to help me forsake it completely. I thank you for your forgiveness, in Jesus' name. I come before your throne of grace boldly, and covered in the shed blood of your Son. In the name of Jesus The Christ, I ask you to cut any and all ungodly soul ties between myself and anyone else [say NAME or NAMES, if appropriate, and the sexual act or acts] created by sexual acts known or unknown, remembered or forgotten.

Please Father God, take the Sword of the Holy Spirit and separate my human spirit from the human spirits of anyone whom I have had ungodly sexual contact. In Jesus' name, I ask You to cleanse those ties by the blood of Jesus of any possible access through which satan can hinder me or my family. "By the authority of the name of the Lord Jesus The Christ, I break the power of any and all covenants, contracts, dedications or commissions made over me (or my children, if any). I seek forgiveness from my wife and ask you, Father God, to put us back in one accord in the name of Jesus Christ the Lord. I now in the name of Jesus The Christ, command any and all demons which may have come into me by ungodly soul ties or any other sin to leave me at once, never to return. I bind all demonic strongholds together as one, and say to them, 'I weaken you with the Blood of Jesus. I command you to go where Jesus Christ The Lord tells you to go by the voice of His Holy Spirit.

' Father God, in Jesus' mighty name, I ask you to shut any doorways of demonic access opened into my life by ungodly soul ties or any other sort of sexual sin, and I ask you to seal those doorways forever with the Blood of the Lamb, shed on the cross of Calvary. I thank you for doing this, in Jesus' name, Amen.

    If your husband is not truly heartbroken for his actions, and only wants to be free of his guilt, then this prayer will not lead to change. In order to experience a true change of heart and behavior, your husband must not be merely worried about facing consequences for his polluted behavior, but must be able to say this prayer with a broken and contrite heart and follow all the steps of accountability. If not, then you must face that fact and begin to move into a place where you can be healed, set free and delivered from all that you have endured. Yes, it's hard but a good soldier can and will endure hardship (see 2 Timothy 2:3).

Keeping It Real: When Infidelity Strikes

Free To Be

Mirror, mirror what do you see?

I see the beauty God created you to be.

No more bondage no more chains

No more sorrow you are free!

Move beyond the hurt the pain

learn to forgive and love again.

To feel a touch that means so much,

Start over make new friends.

Mirror, mirror what do you see?

You cannot erase or change the past

And the future is not yours to hold.

But there is a love so pure and true

Yes, a love that's good as gold.

Mirror, mirror what do you see?

Vivid memories still passing through your mind.

For you are human made of flesh and blood

healing process does take time.

Mirror, mirror what do you see?

You'll find happiness once again

the laughter and kind spoken words

To wipe away the tears.

Hello ME

Begin to ask yourself what you are getting out of your relationship if you know it is infected. Ask yourself where God is in all of this. You don't need to know the answers to these questions right away. Just meditate on them and ask God to give you the answers. And when you are ready, Holy Spirit will lead you into making a decision to be strong in a different way and stay with your spouse, or to be strong and leave your spouse. Now let's get one thing clear. I will never tell anyone to leave his or her spouse. Only Holy Spirit can direct you. Whatever the case may be, Jesus will be there. His word says, "*I will never leave you nor forsake you*" (Deuteronomy 31:6).

Often times we stay in bad relationships because we feel guilty or don't want to leave our spouse in a bad financial, emotional, or social situation. Did he think about you when he was running with the dogs, sleeping with the snakes, telling you lies, hitting and verbally or physically abusing you and not wanting to get help? I know it's a bit harsh... *but I'm just keeping it real.*

We always think *maaaybe* this one time he will change. Nope! This is misplaced guilt and irrational reasoning! Don't let negative emotions like fear of people's opinions, criticism, being alone, guilt or shame keep you in bondage to an infected relationship. Yes, I understand that sometimes leaving a relationship can be like breaking an addiction; it's so hard to break away. Questions flood through your mind. How long must I endure these feelings? When does the pain stop? When does the shame end?

How do I keep my flesh under control? When does the crying stop? After all, he said he was sorry again and he loves me.

No matter how sorry your spouse is afterward, love is never about demeaning or hurting another person. If you have tried everything to save your relationship and it just doesn't work, do not fall into the trap of thinking *you* have to change! Sometimes the only thing that needs changing is your circumstances, and you do have the power to make those changes.

I'm not saying that right now you must forget; that will come with time. Only Jesus can heal the heart, and move bad memories from your mind. I always tell people to look at the spirit that is operating in a person and not the actual person. When you can separate the two, then you are on your way to forgiving that person, and healing can take place.

The reason bitterness gets into a person's heart is that they never resolve the hurt, the pain, or the abuse. They cannot separate the flesh from the spirit, and the result is that bitterness grows, and distrust builds a wall around their heart to the point that everyone they encounter becomes a suspect of their hurt.

Once a person is hurt in a relationship, they may not want to be involved with anyone else for fear of the same thing happening again, especially if there was no true closure to the relationship or understanding of the reasons for its end.

What you must remember is that God created everyone as individuals, and that what happens in one relationship cannot be held against someone else in another relationship. That's why it is so important to be healed inside out.

Keeping It Real: When Infidelity Strikes

If you are not totally healed, no matter what future relationship you become involved in, the minute that person does something which reminds you of your experience in the previous relationship, red flags and all the artillery will rise up inside of you, and it is very possible that there is not even an issue that needs to be addressed. It is very possible that the person you are involved with has done nothing wrong, and you need to do a self-check.

On the other hand, if you do get involved with someone else, make sure that he knows your self-worth. You are worthy to be treated as a lady, respected, loved and honored. Lying, cheating and game playing have no place in your life.

You must realize that being hurt is an escapable part of life because we live in a sinful world. Somewhere, sometime in life, somebody is going to hurt you; the issue becomes how you deal with the hurt. Remember that Jesus stands with open arms waiting to heal you.

He tells us that He will carry our heavy burdens (see Matthew 11: 28-30). God loves you. He will bind up all your wounds and gently remove all your scars so that you can get your fire back! You can be made whole and happy once again, and even have peace with those who hurt you. I know this to be true because I am living it!

If you make the choice to remove yourself from your marriage, it does not mean you don't love the person or care about that person. It does not mean you are a bad person and God is going to punish you, as some would say. What it means is that you will simply no longer allow yourself to be a part of an unhealthy relationship. God has created you to have life and to have it more abundantly; therefore you choose "life."

The Choice

Now that you made a choice to be free from physical and mental bondage of an infected environment, it's time for you to get your value back. Remember you are beautiful--fearfully, wondrously and marvelously made. God created you to both give and receive love. There is no one else like you because God created you unique. You lost your identity due to your circumstances. You lost your identity trying to be who your spouse wanted you to be; you became someone you don't even know. Now it's time to rediscover yourself. Think about what drives your moral compass, brings you strength, what values contribute to your sense of worth and your life philosophy. Consider your beliefs about God and your spiritual life as well as your beliefs about yourself: what messages you send mentally, physically, and emotionally about who you are. Look at your beliefs about life, how you fit into the world, your purpose, attitude, outlook, and the character traits you value.

Find yourself and love yourself! Get your value back! Say this with me... *"I am beautifully and wondrously made. God created me, and everything God created is good and very good, and therefore I am good! I have the mind of Christ Jesus. No longer will I be held in bondage to the actions of (say your spouse's name). I release myself from all pain, worry and hurt that has come into my life, in Jesus' name. I place (say the name) at the feet of Jesus. I forgive (say the name) for all the hurt, pain, and emotional damage he has caused me to walk in."*

If you have children, say this: *"Father God, thank you that my children are not used as tools between (say the name) and me. They are free from all emotional bondage and all generational curses. I thank you, Father, that their marriages are blessed, and their children's marriages are blessed, and their children's children's marriages are blessed by you."*

Keeping It Real: When Infidelity Strikes

Father God, I ask you to forgive me for all hurtful or harsh words and emotional damage I have caused (say the name) in my moments of weakness. Remove all anger and bitterness from my heart, soul, spirit and mind. I thank you, Lord, that you know my heart and that you see all things, and that you have a purpose and plan for my life.

I choose now in the name of Jesus The Christ to walk in love and forgiveness. I realize that I don't have to like the sin or sins of (say the name) but that I must still love him as a person. Today is the beginning of a new day, and today I am made whole in Jesus' name, amen."

If you need to, write your ex-spouse a letter, forgiving him for the hurt and pain that he caused you. Release him; let him go with love so that you are totally free to *be*. As you let him go with love, it removes the yoke of bondage off of him and allows God to work in his life. It removes the yoke of bondage off of you and allows you to move forward. Now, you should feel much better. Begin to picture yourself free.

Creation

Isaiah 42: 5

Thus says God The Lord,

Who created the heavens and stretched them out,

Who spread forth the earth and that which comes from it,

Who gives breath to the people on it

And spirit to those who walk on it:

Isaiah 40:12

Who has measured the waters in the hollow of His hand,

Measured heaven with a span

And calculated the dust of the earth in a measure?

Weighed the mountains in scales

And the hills in a balance

Jeremiah 1:5

Before I formed you in the womb, I knew you

Beauty Inside Out

Man is a spirit who possesses a soul and lives in a body created by God. You have overcome a lot. Now it's time for you to take care of your spirit, mind soul, and body; it's time for you to live from the inside out. Remember you have been living your life for someone else; therefore, you really don't know who you are. Ask yourself these questions: *Who am I? What is my purpose? Where do I want to live? What do I want to be doing? Who do I want loving me, and whom do I want to be loving?*

Focus on your purpose and goals. Since you really don't know the answers to these questions, and to keep from falling into any infected environment ever again, ask God His purpose and plan for your life. Whatever He tells you, write it down. Put it before you and pray over it daily, and it will motivate, uplift and give you strength to do whatever you need to do, and the vision will surely come into full manifestation. Life is a gift given to each and every one of us by the grace of Almighty God, Who made us in His own image. So enjoy life. Begin to see yourself as God sees you, which is beautiful. Look inside yourself and find the beauty, and then bring that beauty outside yourself and share it with others.

Appreciate your uniqueness. You are a beautiful individual with your own personality and talents. Only by appreciating your potential will you be able to nurture your gifts and offer something to the world. Maintain your integrity; don't do anything you might regret later, or you will lose your self-respect. Be honest and ethical, but most importantly have some back bone! Stand up for what's right. No one has a right to treat you with disrespect. If someone puts you down, be your own knight in shining armor!

Respect yourself and your body. Think twice about what you put into your body. Drinking alcoholic beverages, smoking cigarettes, taking drugs and eating unhealthy food should all be eliminated. Oh yes, and be very careful if and when you engage in sexual activity. The last thing you want to do after coming through your process is to jump into another infected relationship. Let God be your husbandman. Get into His presence and let Him be your primary relationship. Let Him create a new you no matter how long it takes. Separate yourself as much as you can for a season and be open to hear God speak. Fast, pray and meditate on His word.

Keep a Journal. There is no certain way to write in a journal, but write in it as often as you can. Write your reflections on your relationships and experiences, good and bad. It's amazing what you will learn about yourself and situations. It will also increase your communication with God. When you go back later and read what you have written, you'll be surprised how blessed you really are.

Be Confident. Even if some days you may find yourself a little down, remain hopeful. Find within yourself what you can do to come into yourself and be happy. I love to dance, I love music, and I am a worshipper. Therefore, when the pressure of life is upon me, I dance, I worship, and I escape in the sound of music. When I finish, I have overcome the things around me, and I see things from a different perspective. Remember God did not bring you out of your process without having a plan for you. Share your testimony; let someone else know that they can make it through their process just as you did. Change your hair, fix it the way you want to. Yes, it *is* all about you. Go shopping for a new wardrobe. If you need to lose a few pounds, exercise and eat right. Get your fire back! Don't do it for anyone else but yourself. Listen to some inspirational jazz, or whatever music you like.

Renew your mind by taking every thought captive to the obedience of The Lord Jesus Christ. Pamper yourself, and that includes your entire being.

Try new things. Whenever the opportunity arises to do something interesting that you've never tried before, do it! Go hiking, skiing, or try a new restaurant. Doing something you've never done before will give you new experiences and make you a more balanced person, and will also get you in the habit of becoming a life-long learner.

Develop a special talent. Is there something that you really wanted to do but did not have the opportunity? Do it! (Exercise good judgment, of course.) Be free! Every day for 15-30 minutes, do something you have always had the passion to do. I love music, and I love to dance so my passion is to go take ballroom, tango, and Latin dancing. So find what it is that you have a passion for and have fun doing it. Day by day, your faith in yourself will begin to rise. You will begin not only to think but to *know* that you are victorious, that you are worthy to be loved and to give love. Day by day you will know more deeply that you are worthy to be respected and treated the way God desires for you to be. You will begin to see yourself as royalty just the way God sees you (see 1st Peter 2:9).

Once God releases you back into the world, begin to surround yourself with people who are on the move for God--people who are God-centered and focus driven, people who truly have the heart of God.

Find people who have made it successfully by walking in purpose and who know who they are and where they are going. Look for people who will build you up in the Christian faith; who will help you get to where God wants you to be. Then, be prepared to do the same thing for them. The word of God says iron sharpens iron (Proverbs 27:17). Have fun, enjoy life in Jesus the Christ!...the next second in life or our next gulp of air is not promised.

Unity

Surrounded by your Glory saturated with your love

Healed and made whole anointed from above.

Who gives us such great gifts as far as I can see

Only you Jesus who lives in me.

Every breathe that we have taken is given by your grace

Every move that we make is order by your love

Who gives us such great gifts as far as I can see

Only you Jesus who lives in me.

Today's a new beginning old things have passed away.

No longer looking back over all the yesterdays

For tomorrow is not promised the future is not ours to hold

So we embrace and trust in you Oh Lord

New life now unfolds.......

Complete Healing and Restoration

Because you have spent time at the feet of Jesus The Christ, because you have forgiven and been forgiven, because you have let go and let Holy Spirit do a work in you, Jesus has healed you. And now you are ready for God to send you your Boaz, your faithful, true husbandman, hand-picked, molded and shaped by God just for you. Who is Boaz one might ask? Well, I will tell you who Boaz was and share with you how Boaz exists today.

After going through the process of healing and being restored . I begin to pray and ask God for my husband because I still believed in the covenant of marriage. Whenever someone would ask me if I would get married again my answer would be, "Only if God drops him in my lap or sends him knocking on my door where I live. I'll never forget It. January 2012, I was in prayer talking to God about my mate and he spoke to me and said, " Get ready, prepare yourself, your Boaz is on the way." I laugh and said, " what God?" Then He said " I'm serious get ready prepare yourself and you will know" Now I must admit while in preparation the counterfeits did come and I almost got caught-up believing that it was a God thing. Well, he looked like, walked like, smelled like, so on, and so forth. Oops! Counterfeit. Not who God had for me...

In one moment, he was there, one glance into each other's eyes and we knew. God speaks. Was it an audible voice that I heard? Soft-spoken word? No, just a knowing, an inner thought that captivated the time and space of that moment. Yes, Lord, I've prayed for such a husbandman. But right here? Right now? Where circumstances and situations are not right? But this deep overwhelming joy, that's bubbling up inside of me with such excitement and amazement, because I know that he is my God-sent husband...

Boaz for me came while I was serving as a Bereavement Coordinator / Chaplain for a Hospice organization -- a place where I least expected to meet my soul mate. My husband's sister was one of our patient's and he just happened to be at his sister's bedside. When I walked into the room, I knew immediately that he was the one. Likewise, he knew I was the one for him. Our eyes unpretentiously met. We had conversation concerning his sister then I curiously left the room.

Strangely enough Holy Spirit begin to impress upon me about this man I knew nothing about. I begin to say to God, "This man's sister is dying how does that make me look?" Now, who am I to question what, where and how God does a thing. So what did I do? I submitted, I said yes Lord. And now today I can say thank you Lord for my Boaz, my husband, my best friend. You too will also be able to say the same thing. Now let's take a look at Ruth and Boaz...

The book of Ruth in the Bible is not by any means a love story to find a husband. I am using this book as a metaphor to show the love Boaz had for God., his character, integrity, generosity and care he had towards Ruth and wrapping it all into the fact that some men today do poses those same qualities and characteristics.

The time and culture in the book of Ruth is much different and people married for other reasons in that day than we do now. This story of Ruth and Boaz shows us just how much God loves us, and always wants restoration for His people. With that being said let's take a look at Boaz....

He is Worthy

Boaz was described as a worthy man (Ruth 2:1) who believed in the Lord (Ruth 2:4)

Today's Boaz will have a good reputation because he's proven himself to be a man of character and worth by his actions. . He will have a solid relationship with the Lord. He will not just look like a Christian, his life style will be a reflection of Christ. You will be equally yoked in your relationship, with each person growing in their faith, serving the Lord, and the fruit of the Holy Spirit will be evidence.

He is Observant

Ruth caught Boaz's eye (Ruth 2:5), but he also noticed her inward character, good deeds (Ruth 2:11-12), and kindness (Ruth 3:10). When Boaz first shows up in his barley field outside the walls of Bethlehem, he notices Ruth immediately. He turns to his foreman and asks, "Whose young woman is that?"

Today's Boaz He's looking at you. He will find you attractive! He will attach importance to your inner beauty. He will notice the qualities in you. He will learn of you to find out what makes you tick, and seek to understand you more fully with time. He will notice what you enjoy. He will take pleasure in making you laugh and smile. He will be so in tune with you that the slightest change in your emotions, body language, hair, tone of voice he will notice.

He is a Protector

Boaz encouraged Ruth to glean in his own field, so that she would be safe among the other women. He also charged the young men of his field not to touch her (Ruth 2:9).

Today's Boaz knows that sex is a sacred act to be enjoyed only in marriage, and he appreciates your high standards. He will protect your purity, as well as his own, by respecting boundaries. You will know where he stands. He won't lead you on by just "hanging out" with you for an extended period of time, enjoying the benefits of your company without accepting appropriate responsibility toward you.

He is a Provider

Boaz met Ruth's needs. He gave her plenty of water to drink (Ruth 2:9), provided meals for her (Ruth 2:14), and gave her an abundance of barley to share with Naomi (Ruth 3:15).

Today's Boaz will work hard. He is a mature, responsible man with right priorities. Being a provider is not about making lots of money. It's about a man meeting the basic needs of his wife and children.

He understands a man's Biblical role as the leader of the household. You will feel safe and secure as his wife. This is because he has your best interests in mind, serves you sacrificially, and loves you as Christ loved the church.

He is Compassionate

Boaz had care and concern for others, loving his neighbor as himself. As the owner of a field, Boaz showed generosity and compassion on the less fortunate by following Levitical law (Leviticus 19:9-10).

Today's Boaz will Look for opportunities to bless others. Serve wholeheartedly; give generously, as God prompts him to do so. He cherishes family and friends. He is kind and loving to the "littlest and least," not looking down on others in self-righteousness. Utilize his spiritual gifts to edify the body of believers and honor God.

He is a Man of Integrity

Boaz knew that there was a closer relative who had "first dibs" in redeeming Ruth (Ruth 3:12-13). He took the proper steps (Ruth 4:1-6) to win her hand in marriage. In fact, he couldn't even rest until the matter was properly settled (Ruth 3:18). Boaz also had witnesses (Ruth 4:9) to confirm that he acted with integrity.

Today's Boaz does not manipulate, cheat, or lie. He has nothing to hide. Does what is right, even when it's hard: Respects the authorities in his life; Heeds the wise counsel of a more seasoned Christian man, such as a pastor or mentor, who will come alongside him, ask tough questions, hold him accountable, and encourage him in Christ-likeness. That's today's Boaz and that is whom God The Father sent to me.

The word of God says, *He that findeth a wife findeth a good thing* (Proverbs 18:22). You don't have to go looking for a husband, but position yourself to be found, but be careful because counterfeits will come so you must know what to look for. While you wait, get out and mingle, find art galleries, plays, music festivals, multi-cultural and international events, etc....you get my point. God knows your heart's desires, and he will bring them to the fullness in time. Watch and wait; your Boaz is on the way.

Just a few key points to remember: When you meet your Boaz, keep it real; don't be fake trying to put your best foot forward. Be who you really are. Remember God made you over. Communication is a two-way street so don't be so anxious that you over-talk. Listen to what he has to say. Find out his interests, his likes and dislikes, and find out if you are on the same page, meaning are you looking for the same thing. One major factor should be whether he has a personal relationship with Jesus The Christ. Does he love the Lord with all his heart, soul and mind? If the answer is yes, then he will have no problem treating you the right way.

Whatever you do or say, do not put him in the same boat as your ex-spouse. Understand your Boaz is not your ex, and you have forgiven your ex and moved forward, so don't rewind the past or hold yourself and your Boaz in captivity. Get a clear understanding of any boundaries that may exist. In a new relationship, sometimes things don't take off so fast. There may be areas that are not open for conversation right away, but as you get to know each other, those areas will open up.

Sex in a relationship is often compared to a car. It is often said that you don't buy a car without first test driving it. Well, remember you are not looking for sex, but a relationship. And you definitely are not a car! *(hey, just keeping it real)*. Keep a clean heart and keep the flesh under control. Don't jump into bed.

Have you ever seen the movie Forrest Gump? In that movie Forrest's girl Jenny is always saying to Forrest when trouble comes, "run, Forrest, run!" and Forrest takes off running as fast as he can. Likewise, I say to you when you see fornication (sex without marriage) coming your way,

Keeping It Real: When Infidelity Strikes

RUN! If it looks like sex without connection and relationship, RUN! I know, everyone is having sex, and the society makes it look so good, and yes, it feels so good, but hey, I'm *just keeping it real*. Remember what happens afterwards? The "soul ties." Yikes! Here's what I've come to realize: When all is said and done, when our life has come to an end, certainly we want to hear the voice of the Lord say, "Well done."

In an Instant

Life is short in this temporary world

There is so much to do and see

If we keep an open mind

God unfolds His mysteries

Don't let circumstance and situations get in your way

Or you may miss the very words

God is trying to say.

We never know what God is doing

Or whom He may use

To help a person through the toughest times

Be ready He may use you.

Life is short in this temporary world

Live it with no regrets

For death comes to us all

But we will live again

And again we shall live

Life is short in this temporary world

Embrace pure love

With the one God sends you....

Keeping It Real: When Infidelity Strikes

Today's Boaz Speaks

For me (The Boaz), reading this book was like hitting the rewind button of the infidelity I have experienced in my life. In society when infidelity strikes we naturally think that it's the husband or boyfriend when this happens, but in my case, it was the wife. During that period, most of the heartbreak I experienced was kept a secret. For a long time I would act as if everything was fine when around my friends. I especially kept it from my parents (my mother in particular) because I didn't want to upset them. If I didn't have a personal relationship with God, things would have surely spiraled out of control in a bad way.

I am very excited to be a part of this book, because I think it really tells a story of what many people both female and male alike go through in life. I was very content with my (single) life the way it had been for the past 15 years. I had not resigned myself to never getting married again, but I had decided that the only way it would happen was if God sent me someone.

One day while visiting my sister Melanie, who was a patient at a Hospice facility due to breast cancer, I met Christine (My Ruth in biblical terms). She came up to me on the second day that I was there and offered to show me around the facility. Even though the timing was not ideal, due to the reason I was there, I was completely drawn to her. From that very first encounter, our conversations seem to flow so free and easy. And every day after that, I found myself hoping that she would come by my sister's room and if she didn't I was very disappointed.

At that point, I was thinking that God had finally sent me the person he intended me to be with. I think Melanie had a feeling that something very special was about to happen with us too. I say this because one day while visiting my sister, the nurses at the Hospice facility wanted to give her a bath. Melanie at this point thought that there was no reason to get one because she felt her life was over. My mother, who had been bathing her for about a week since her arrival, could not convince her to take one. Not even Melanie's daughter could get her to take a bath and Melanie was very adamant about it too. Along comes Christine, and she begin to calmly talk to her. Melanie looked at me and then back at Christine and after a minute or two, she agreed to take a bath. God was playing the role of cupid with Christine and I and I feel that Melanie could sense it too.

Melanie passed away on her 12th day in the hospice facility and that was one of the most difficult periods in my family's life as well as my own. Christine and I continued to see each other. She even came to Melanie's funeral. At this point, she and I had become so close that we already knew that we wanted to spend the rest of our lives together even though we had only known each other about three weeks.

1 Corinthians, 7th Chapter, 9th verse says, "If an unmarried man and woman cannot exercise self-control, let them marry." For it is better to marry than to burn with passion. Most of our friends thought we were moving much too fast; Christine and I were married a little more than a month after we met.

Keeping It Real: When Infidelity Strikes

Christine has truly been a blessing in my life and our relationship continues to grow both spiritually and personally. I had thought I was happy with my life before I met her, but I was only fooling myself because now I truly know what real happiness feels like. She has a true calling as a Minister and is an awesome servant of God. Christine and I pray together daily and I feel really close and so much love for her during those moments. Every day we spend together has been exciting and we just thank God for bringing us together. Life is so short in this temporary world we live in and I am so glad that I get to spend the rest of my time here with my Ruth.

Thanks, Melanie. Rest in peace.

The Sound

There is a Rhythm in The Sound that changes The Atmosphere.

When we are walking to The Rhythm

Whenever we enter into wherever we go,

The Atmosphere changes to The Sound of The Rhythm.

The Sound is God's Voice!

The Rhythm is Jesus' Heart beat!

The Atmosphere is Holy Spirit's Presence!

Women of Great Value

This section is about women who made it through all their trials and tribulations. They made it through all their heartache and pain, and found joy, peace and laughter. They are walking "Victorious Women on the Move." They are Women of Great Value & Integrity because The Father, The Son and The Holy Spirit direct their path.

As women of worth, we have value, beauty, and confidence, and we demonstrate these in everything we do. As women of great value, we make a difference and change the world around us everywhere we go because we are walking to the sound!

What does it mean to be a Woman of Worth? It means that we are women that know who we are in Christ Jesus, and we don't base our value on the opinions of others. We know how to be a great help to our spouse if we have one, but yet independent and intelligent enough to make our own way. We are women of worth who base our value totally upon who the word of God says we are. The word of God says we are fearfully and wonderfully made and that our value has been set far above rubies. (See Psalm 139:14; Proverbs 31:10; and Deuteronomy 32-10:12.) We are also the apple of God's eye, and when He looks at us, He calls us beautiful.

As women of great value we don't live in resentment but walk in forgiveness. We let others know that we love them but not their sin. We are always looking for reconciliation and opportunity to witness about the love of The Lord Jesus Christ.

We don't gossip or give into busyness. We are always seeking God so that we can move to the next level in Him, to build up His Kingdom as we walk in purpose. As women of great value, we know how to encourage other women and appreciate their uniqueness without being jealous or envious.

As you share in the testimonies of these women, may you find yourself free to flow with every fiber of your being and embrace your new sound.

Keeping It Real: When Infidelity Strikes

Women On The Move

Danyele's Story

I was married for 21years and found out that my husband was picking up prostitutes off the streets and bringing them to our home. He was having wild sex while videotaping himself. I left home and moved into an apartment. He had a stroke and I moved back in to take care of him. I went to work one day and was led to come home on my lunch break, which is something I never did, and to my horrific surprise, I found my husband and three prostitutes at our home having a wild sex party. That was the last straw! Even when you can't see "the forest for the trees," God will show you signs to let you know something's wrong. God allowed my husband a chance to change his ways, but he kept going down that same road. He had another stroke and another. God showed him enough is enough. I tried to make my marriage work, but I realized the very thing you are trying to hold on to, God is saying to let it go. It reminds me of "the children of Israel" wanting to go back to Egypt. It was easy in Egypt; Pharaoh gave the slaves everything. The result was that they became totally dependent on him and were held back from living the life of promise. Don't go back to Egypt! I'm still standing and keeping it real!

Gutzmore's Story

Beloved, this is my testimony to tell of a God who carried me through the worst six years of my life. After my divorce I thought I was in control of my destiny. I could handle all the trials and tribulations that we're accruing in my life. In the past I was successful and did it all by myself so now what's the difference? With issues coming at me from left and right, I could figure my way out of every situation and solve my problems. Yes! I prayed to God for a solution; but I did not leave the solutions up to him. I was doing the thinking, trying to borrow money from friends; maxed out on all my credit cards; mortgage in arrears; IRS putting liens on all my possessions.

Beloved, I prayed day and night. I cried on my way to work. I cried when I was alone. I cried at nights, asking God why all this is happening to me. I would give the last piece of bread I had to someone in need. Always there for family and friends and now there is no one to help me. But GOD was always there carrying me through my storm.

My reality came when an agent from the IRS came to seize my car, looked at me and said "I see you are a hard working lady, come and see me at my office." As I was driving home that evening I started crying and a voice said close your eyes and just drive into oncoming traffic. Which I did, when a voice yelled at me to open my eyes, Jesus! Jesus! I opened my eyes just in time to turn the steering away from the car that I was about to hit head on. That moment I began to thank, praise and worship God for saving my life. I told God I could not solve these problems; he had to do it for me.

Keeping It Real: When Infidelity Strikes

With the help of a dear friend and mentor who was always interceding for me, prayed with me and reminded me I serve a God who delights in seeing me prosper. He is Jehovah Jireh and I should stand on his promises and claim them (Psalm 37:25). I have never seen the righteous forsaken, or his seed begging for bread.

Beloved, all I could do at this stage of my life was to put my faith and trust in Christ Jesus then begin to walk in his Grace (unmerited Favor) the doors of heaven opened and miracles started to happen. Debts begin to be cancelled, my mortgage came out of foreclosure and my interest rate lowered. Without refinancing the IRS closed my file. I am now an ordained Minister preaching The Gospel of Jesus Christ. *God sent me a Boaz!* I've remarried. Yes, there are still waves, but I am walking on water because I have learned to keep my eyes steadfast on Christ Jesus who is constant, loving and ever faithful.

God bless you my sister and much success with your book. May it be a light to the dark path of those who are walking in the darkness.

Proverbs 31 Woman's Story

I gave my all in the marriage. My ex-spouse, a minister, proclaimed God told him, that I was the one, his wife. Then after the I do's our conversations just became short or non-existent. I wanted my marriage to work. Beforehand I was always praying saying to God that I want to be that Proverbs 31 woman and like every woman. I wanted to be married. After getting married I wasn't what my mate wanted -- he wanted another man. I met my ex-spouse at a retail store where I had been the manager for 20 years. We lived in different locations and when I married him I didn't quit my job. I would just commute a daily two hour drive until I got days off work to go home where my hubby was for the week-end.

During those times I still had wifely duties so when I came home on Saturdays after getting off work. I would stay there until Monday mornings, so looking forward to seeing him. Once there, we would watch TV, not much to talk about at all. It had even come to a point him asking why I don't watch TV in the other room. My mate had three close friends that were females. I would tell him that shouldn't be and if they can't be close to me, your wife, then they shouldn't be your close friends. I had only one close guy friend whom I put aside for my ex-hubby. I really loved my husband I even had a little name I would call him. He appeared to like it but around others he couldn't stand it. He became a very different individual.

One of the main things that I did as a wife was to make sure my ex-husband had clean clothes from week to week. Before returning to work, I would cook breakfast, lunch, and dinner. I would cook a breakfast casserole of some sort, and seven to eight dishes for lunch and dinner, his request,

Keeping It Real: When Infidelity Strikes

most of the time. Maybe a month into this marriage, arguments became hot, no conversations. He didn't want me to come home except only on Sunday's just to be a trophy. I would iron his clothes for the entire week, lay them out, have them together from the socks that matched to the under garments all the way down to his shoes. The only thing he honestly had to do was to take a shower and put his attire on every day. I even laid out a bonus outfit so if he left the house after coming in he had something other than work attire to put on. Still, to him, that seemed not to be good enough. I was the bread winner, so, I would leave him money to fill the car up for gas or to pay bills and sometimes both. It wasn't a big deal to me, after all he was my husband. Whatever I could do to take pressure off our situation or make him feel at ease I felt like I needed to do it.

I was by his side at church, remember he is a minister. We would get home from church and he would not talk to me at all. I would be in one room crying and he would shut the door so he could not hear me. When we would talk, he would tell me he didn't marry me because he loved me, he married me for stability. Stability? Now, that really took the cake. I continue to pray, "Lord he said you put us together how with all this turmoil, you are a God of peace?" So here I am still working, ironing his clothes, cooking, cleaning, my wifely duties and so on. One weekend we went to the movies. In this movie Janet Jackson finds out her husband is gay. In the movie she becomes HIV positive. So, when we get home getting ready for bed we were talking about the movie. I ask my ex-hubby had a man ever tried him. He said yes. I asked, "Have you ever done anything?" He stated no. After his answer he wouldn't look at me. He balled up, turned in the opposite direction from facing me. As I was talking to him he just didn't look right. I already had my suspicions, but I said in my mind like everything else I'll let it go for a minute. My husband already didn't like having sex with me. He would ejaculate in bed with me lying right beside him. I would even ask, "Why are you doing that when I am right here?" He would state "It takes too long for us. Now I'm crying, "baby, baby." Yet still, I was ignored. A week later I started acting like I wanted him so bad. I even went to, well, I'm ashamed to say this but.... a part of his body where most men would slap your head off if you even suggested such a thing. As Christine would say, *"hey just keeping it real."* Anyway, I entered one finger he moaned, entered two same thing moaning. I went for the third finger. All at one time his legs went straight up! My mouth flew open. Oh my gosh! All my questions were answered. The next day my ex-husband asked why did I do that. I told him because I thought you might like it. He said he did.

    I knew my ex-husband was gay, yet he had been with me. Time went on, arguments got worse -- we actually got into a fist fight and everything changed. The little church he was going to, they knew but kept quiet. Things got unbearable I pack my stuff in my car and left. When I went back to get the rest of my belongings he had changed the locks on the door. Upon trying to get into the house, he was in there, heard me and he called the cops and said I was trying to break in. 4 police cars pulled up, all I could say is I stay here. They told me if I didn't leave they would take me to jail, so I left.

Keeping It Real: When Infidelity Strikes

As of this day have not got back everything I lost. I said all of that to say this. **_Ladies "keep it real"_** as Christine would say, with yourself. Please do not overlook any signs that you see in your mate that give you a red flag…that makes you say hmmm. They are always caution signs, bumps, eye openers to take a deeper look into what is really being happening. If it does not look right, chances are it isn't. Listen to that small, inner voice. Never will God give you less than you deserve. As women we all deserve a real man! Anything less will not do. I am not yet even thinking about marriage right now.

I've been divorced for three years. Only recently, have I started to date. I'm taking it very slowly. Believing God gives back double for my troubles. Most of all I am in good health. I get an HIV test done every six months to a year. God is an awesome God! Greater is coming. God prepares us for greater things. Be strong God is able. Much love!

Jewel's Story

I experienced a feeling of loss and helplessness for years and it was all due to the perceived obstacles in my life. I use the term perceived because at the time I did not have a relationship with my heavenly father. I knew of him but I had not become his bride. Like most believers, I attended church, read my Bible regularly, prayed daily, taught Sunday school, and I served on the usher board at church. I knew the word, but the word had not yet become nutrition for my soul.

I married twice and divorced twice. The first time I married for security and the second time for love. Love for me was an emotional high with high expectations for that special man in my life. It was an attraction and it felt good as long as things were going well. I finally had it right and surely this love would last forever, but after four years things started to go downhill. He became verbally abusive, started cheating and we literally started to live separate lives. I was married but lonely, which propagated resentment, and anger. I tried but failed to communicate to my spouse my feelings and needs. He refused counseling. I had to come to the realization that our relationship and marriage had crumbled beyond repair and the love and attraction we once felt for each other had dissipated. By the time we divorced, I was emotionally and physically drained. It was during this time that my relationship with my Heavenly Father grew. I learned to pray the word of GOD with expectations and thanksgiving. His holy words set me free from my anger, pain, resentment and I began to feel and sense his presence and gradually the loneliness disappeared. I was obedient and prayed his word, asking for his guidance and in him. I found peace, joy, unconditional love and freedom from condemnation.

Keeping It Real: When Infidelity Strikes

When I look back over my journey, I have to smile and praise GOD for my deliverance. If I were to offer any advice to other women who are going through a transition it would be to seek godly friends who love you and will pray with you and for you. Love yourself, put your faith and trust in GOD, live in the moment and be patient. Know that you are "loved and wonderfully made in his image" and he always hears when you call.

Love to all my sisters. "Today is new, make the most of it and use it wisely."

Spiritual Warrior's Story

Hurt, rejection, disappointment, and heartaches come in different forms and ways. I experienced it through years of sexual promiscuity. When I was a young girl an older man took advantage of my innocence hence started the deception from the enemy that my body was supposed to be given to men for their pleasure. It was implanted in my mind the only way to express my feelings towards them was to give myself sexually to them. Every man with whom I was interested required sex from me. I don't know if it was something written on me that I was damaged goods, easy, or maybe it was my appearance as I was this skinny little dark skinned girl with acne. So when the guys showed interest in me I thought it was real because I wanted it to be...not knowing all they wanted from me was sex and to become another one of their conquests.

As I got older I had a need to satisfy my flesh for by now my sexual emotions were fully open and I desired sexual relationships even if it was for only a one night stand, at least it was some form of attention. That was the lie Satan wanted me to believe. It took me some time to realize with every encounter; with every man I laid with I was losing a piece of self-worth, self-esteem and respect for myself and from others as I felt everyone knew my secret. It wasn't until early adulthood I learned how I wanted to be treated or how a woman was supposed to be treated, at least I thought. However, this lesson was taught by a married man. Yes, I was one of those "the other woman," hence starting a whole new level of deception and manipulation.

Keeping It Real: When Infidelity Strikes

At first it appeared real to me, wining, dining, gifts, meeting my financial needs, special attention because I was the special one, I was the one he really wanted to be with. How stupid it sounds now but back then it worked for me. **"Just keeping it real."** Then I found myself changing and evolving and my life just took another type of spin on it and the only men I appeared to be attractive to were married men. Don't be fooled my sisters the enemy knows what we want, what we yearn for, and the areas of our lives that are attention-deprived. It took me a minute to realize the married ones had to be good to me how else were they going to hold my attention. And because they could take care of me the way I wanted to be lavished and treated, I went for their lies -- except this time I was gaining more than a five minute thrill.

However, when it is time for God's plan to start working in your life enough becomes enough. One night I ran into Jesus at this little country roadside church and although the preacher God used to usher me into His presence is no longer with us and is resting in the arms of the Lord. God used him to tell me all about myself. That night I felt like the woman at the well. Through God's revealing of my past, what was going on at the present time, and His thoughts for my future I felt ashamed, humiliated, and used on one hand and on the other I knew I had found something different, I felt something inside of me that I had never felt before.

Jesus began to purge me and cleanse me as He began to take everything away from me that was familiar to me. I thought I was going to literally die through that process. It felt like layers were being peeled away from the depths of my being. There was a time when my body would ache so much that it would hurt and burn and all I could do was cry and roll around on my bed wondering when all of this was going to be over and if I would make it through. There was a time when I would just clinch my Bible couldn't even read it; didn't know where to go in the Bible that would speak to what I was going through. There were times I could not open the Bible. I would wake up some mornings in a fetal position with the Bible clinched to my chest and I would cry and thank God for keeping me one more night. Keeping me from making a telephone call to handle that situation ("just keeping it real") as Satan would be in my ear urging me to go for it pick up the telephone God will forgive you this one time. Yes there were a couple of times I did fall and those occurrences happened with me being involved in church, but the enemy doesn't leave you alone because you are in church and some of you sisters, even married ones, know what I mean -- "just keeping it real." However, it was through genuine repentance, determination, and God's constant reminder to me how much He loves me and how He needed me that kept me fighting to stay saved. Yes fighting because the enemy was challenging me on every hand. His plans were not to let me go without a fight. I had to "purpose" in my mind that I wanted to be saved; I wanted to be with the Lord, if He could love me and forgive me with all I had been through and had done, I wanted to be pleasing to Him too.

It was in my personal meditation and worship relationship that I found deliverance and peace. Now some fifteen years later I am free, I am liberated, I have been delivered from unhealthy relationships and sexual promiscuity and will remain this way until my "Boaz" or Jesus -- which every comes first. Just **"keeping it real!!"**

Sisters I hope this testimony sets the captives free as I am still finding more and more liberation in Christ. It is a WONDERFUL thing!!

Keeping It Real: When Infidelity Strikes

Julie Ann's Story: The Testimony of God's Grace

Proverbs 3:5-6 Woman As I began to ask Holy Spirit for His direction on how to share my testimony, considering the title of the book, it first came to me that I had been an unfaithful wife and an unfaithful daughter to our Heavenly Father. I felt compelled to look up the meaning of the word infidelity only to find that the origin and history was "want of faith, unbelief in religion, "unfaithfulness," noun of quality from infidels; meaning "unfaithfulness or disloyalty to a person, lover or a spouse." My research yielded confirmation of the direction Holy Spirit would have me to go.

I was living with the man of my dreams, the man I thought I would marry, only to find myself unhappy and unfulfilled. I began to feel drawn to God, interested in going to church, had a desire to know more about Jesus, and simply wanted more. It wasn't long before I accepted Jesus Christ as my savior, at age 22. I immediately moved out from living with my boyfriend and began to serve God with all of my being, learning all that I could learn of His ways.

The young man who would become my first husband, yes, I said first (as Christine says, just "Keeping it Real"), played the role of a drug dealer in the play at church that led me to Christ. We became the closest of friends. He had been raised in the church and was the purest young man you could ever imagine, but not I! I had a past -- one that I was not too proud of. But I had found new life in my savior, forgiveness for all past sin, a chance to have a fresh new start. Somehow I found myself crossing lines that as a Godly woman I should not be crossing. This is where I began to be unfaithful to my Father, not keeping His commandments.

When we do that, we open the door for things to happen, we, buy our choices, set the wheels in motion for things to come our way. Not always, but often, we are the ones responsible. I became pregnant and yes, I did get married to this sweet, innocent young man. The problem was I wasn't complete within myself in order to give what was needed. I found myself unfulfilled and unfaithful to him, divorced and a single parent. I repeated this pattern of marrying three more times, one of which included my first. Yes, in search of myself, I hurt people all along the journey. In the re-marriage to my first husband, I was yet again unfaithful, knowing fully that God wasn't going to tolerate this behavior; I became pregnant, this time, not by my husband. I sought the direction of a Christian counselor as I found myself extremely distraught and disoriented, all by my own doing, my choices, my actions….he said two things to me that have forever been with me. "Two wrongs don't make a right (don't abort), and the Truth makes you free…you know the rest, you must walk it out!"

You may say, what does that actually mean, well…I knew exactly what it meant. Take responsibility for your choices and don't try to hide or dismiss it. Allow God's truth to expose darkness and disobedience and come back to the fullness of God's truth and life for you. I did just that, I told my husband the truth, I accepted my consequences and God's forgiveness. The biggest problem I had was forgiving myself -- huge problem. It took me a long time. I was so ashamed of myself.

The truth is, I allowed deception to come into my life, and I allowed distractions to enter my focus and then allowed them to direct me down a road that brought a lot of pain to others. My behavior had nothing to do with what my husband wasn't doing that he should be doing. No, not at all…it had everything to do with me, my insecurities, my issues, not his.

Keeping It Real: When Infidelity Strikes

Still, to this day I stand in awe of how God had grace and mercy on me. My heart has always been pure, no ill will toward others. What is absolutely beautiful about my story is God used my weakness, my shortcomings and my failures and blessed me in the midst with a beautiful daughter. She arrived with great purpose and continues to this day to bring joy and healing to all of those lives she touches. The road was not easy and to this day it holds its hurts, like the fact that my precious innocent daughter doesn't know her biological father. The fact that I remarried and allowed this man to adopt her, however he never had a relationship with her. I lived ten years in this marriage determined I would not fail "again" at marriage. In these ten years I became closer to God than I'd ever been; I found my true self, found peace within and became a whole person in Christ. I came to the full understanding that our Savior has all that we will ever need, our joy and happiness comes from within, not from without, that our true peace and contentment comes from Him. This is so LIBERATING, not to attach the responsibility of your joy to another person; it's simply not their job to make you happy.

I gave myself to service to our Lord through youth ministry and women's ministry and later became an ordained minister. After ten years of loneliness, the Lord released me from this marriage. You may say, "how" did He release you…the man I was married to made the statement to me, "you are a good woman, just not the woman for me"! Many would find those words as rejection, but not I. I found them to be freeing because they spoke truth. Truth always makes you free, no matter how much pain. Truth immediately delivers to you; it will ultimately give you freedom if you will embrace it.

I am not sure why God chooses the foolish, but He does. I am one of those. I have many times wondered "how" He (God) could ever use someone like me, but the truth is He will use any and all of us who will submit to and allow Him to use us, all for His glory. God continues to use and bless me abundantly, not because I am of worth, but because He alone is worthy and He dwells within me! I have since married my soul mate, a man who accepts me for who I am, who loves the Jesus in me and loves my daughters and family. I too met my Boaz…blessed and thankful am I.

I pray that no matter where your road has taken you, that you will embrace truth, be true to yourself and allow God to develop His greatness within you. I promise it will be the most liberating experience of a lifetime. He will direct your path if you seek His ways first. Proverbs 3:5-6.

Bio

Dr. Christine Rice Slocumb is a native of Boise, Idaho. She earned her Master of Divinity and Doctorate of Ministry in 2009. Christine is a licensed ordained Minister, Chaplain, and Certified Counselor, and Hospice Bereavement Coordinator. Currently she serves as one of the Associate Pastor of Stubbs Chapel Church in Macon, Georgia.

Christine says it is not the degrees that make a person. It is only when we submit ourselves to God that we know who we are and the full purpose for our life. Her passion is to help people fulfill their calling in life and to walk in freedom! Christine loves music and is a vocalist as well as a song writer who is moved by every aspect of the Arts.

Christine is married with children and resides in the Florida area with her husband.

For Conferences, Grief support Groups or other speaking engagements please contact: (850) 217-8215.

Made in the USA
Charleston, SC
08 February 2015